How Divine Mercy
Heals the Effects of Abortion

Dr. Bryan Thatcher
Eucharistic Apostles of The Divine Mercy

Rev. Frank Pavone
Priests for Life

Marian Press

Congregation of Marians of the Immaculate Conception
Stockbridge, Massachussetts

2003

NIHIL OBSTAT
Rev. Richard Drabik, MIC
CENSOR

IMPRIMI POTEST
Very Rev. Walter M. Dziordz, MIC
Provincial Superior
St. Stanislaus Kostka Province
Congregation of Marians of the Immaculate Conception

The Nihil Obstat is a declaration that a book or pamphlet to be published is considered to be free from doctrinal or moral error. It is not implied that those who have granted the Nihil Obstat agree with the contents, opinions, or statements expressed.

To Obtain Additional Copies of this booklet:
Please call toll-free 1-800-462-7426
Or write to:
Association of Marian Helpers
Eden Hill, Stockbridge, MA 01263

AVAILABLE THROUGH THE MARIAN WEBSITE
at www.marian.org
Call the EADM ministry toll free at 1-877-380-0727
(website at www.thedivinemercy.org)
Call the Priests for Life at 1-718-980-4400
(website at www.priestsforlife.org)

ISBN: 0-944203-83-3
Printed in the United States of America

TABLE OF CONTENTS

In March 2003, the Holy Father imparted his Apostolic Blessing on the Eucharistic Apostles of The Divine Mercy for the ministry's pro-life work. Below is the text of the blessing.

Calling to Remembrance the participation in Our Lord's Agony in Gethsemani of Saint Maria Faustina Kowalska of the Most Blessed Sacrament, who at least thrice in her lifetime willingly accepted the violent pains that convulsed her for three hours and at times caused her to lose consciousness, as allowed by Jesus in order to offer reparation to God for infants murdered in their mothers' wombs (*Diary*, 1276),

To All Members of The Eucharistic Apostles of The Divine Mercy — a Lay Ministry Outreach of the Congregation of Marians of the Immaculate Conception of the Most Blessed Virgin Mary —

And to All the Faithful Worldwide, who join them in offering The Divine Mercy Chaplet — revealed to St. M. Faustina for averting divine chastisement — for mothers, that they not abort their offspring; for infants in danger of being put to death in the womb; for a change of heart of providers of abortions and of their collaborators; for human victims of stem cell research, genetic manipulation, cloning and euthanasia; and for all entrusted with the government of peoples, that they may promote the "Culture of Life" so as to put an end to the "culture of death,"

I impart, as a token of a superabundance of Divine Graces, My Heartfelt Apostolic Blessing.

Given at the Vatican, March, A.D. 2003
Solemnity of the Incarnation of The Divine Word
In the 25th year of My Pontificate — **Joannes Paulus II**

Calling to Remembrance

the participation in Our Lord's Agony in Gethsemani of
Saint Maria Faustina Kowalska of The Most Blessed Sacrament,
who at least thrice in her lifetime willingly accepted the violent pains
that convulsed her for three hours and at times caused her to lose consciousness,
as allowed by Jesus in order to offer reparation to God
for infants murdered in their mothers' wombs (Diary, §1276).

To All Members of
The Eucharistic Apostles of The Divine Mercy
—A Lay Ministry Outreach of the Congregation of Marians
of The Immaculate Conception of The Most Blessed Virgin Mary—
and
To All The Faithful Worldwide, who join them in offering
The Divine Mercy Chaplet
— revealed to St. M. Faustina for averting divine chastisement —
for mothers, that they not abort their offspring;
for infants in danger of being put to death in the womb;
for a change of heart of providers of abortions and of their collaborators;
for human victims
of stem cell research, genetic manipulation, cloning and euthanasia;
and for all entrusted with the government of peoples,
that they may promote the "Culture of Life"
so as to put an end to the "culture of death."

I impart,
as a token of a Superabundance of Divine Graces,
My Heartfelt Apostolic Blessing.

Given at the Vatican, March A.D. 2003,
Solemnity of the Incarnation of The Divine Word
In the 25th year of My Pontificate.

Joannes Paulus II

PREFACE

Will God Forgive Me?

Many know that God is a merciful Savior to others, yet many truly wonder — and doubt — that God could ever forgive them for their own serious sins. They believe that He might lavish His mercy on others, but could never be so merciful to them. For many, abortion is one of those "unforgivable" sins, one so terrible that it nullifies God's unfathomable mercy.

Unfortunately, these people are mired in their own quicksand of doubt, guilt, and shame, as evidenced by the personal witnesses in this booklet of Laura and Joan. They are two good examples of the complications of abortion that ripple through affected families like a stone thrown on the surface of a flat, glassy pond. Abortion is about much more than a simple procedure done on one day and forgotten about the next.

Why a booklet on abortion and God's mercy? We believe it is sorely needed because people who have committed or been a part of this sin need to come to healing and accept the mercy of God in their lives. Many cannot accept the fact that God hates the sin but loves the sinner. We are not attempting to minimize the sin, and realize that nothing can replace the loss of the aborted child. However, to get through the difficult days in life, God's love and compassion need to be felt by all as we traverse this valley of tears.

7

Womb, Not Tomb

In Hebrew, the word for "mercy" shares the same root as the word for "womb." The womb is the place of mercy, where the tiniest, most vulnerable lives are to find unconditional welcome and nurture. God's first act of mercy toward us is that He gives us life. He also calls us to be a people of mercy, giving ourselves in love for one another. Abortion is the very antithesis of mercy. Rather than sacrificing oneself for the other, abortion sacrifices the other for oneself. Yet, in God's plan, mercy is meant to triumph, and so those who have been a part of abortion can also receive God's abundant mercy.

Two essential elements of living the message of mercy are forgiveness, not only of others, but also of oneself, and a deep trust in God. Just as Jesus forgives all repentant sinners, we are to forgive others, and yes, even ourselves. All of us must continually trust in His unfathomable mercy, even those of us who have been involved in abortion. Our Lord told Saint Faustina that He wanted the image of The Divine Mercy to be signed with the words, "Jesus, I trust in You!" Trust is the hallmark of living the message of mercy. Jesus told Saint Faustina, **The graces of My mercy are drawn by means of one vessel only, and that is trust. The more a soul trusts, the more it will receive** (*Diary of Saint Faustina,* 1578). We hope this booklet will help others to end the cycle of shame, guilt, and abuse, and bring healing and closure to all families affected by abortion.

CHAPTER 1
The Lies of Abortion

When *Roe vs. Wade* was decided by the Supreme Court of the United States by a 7–2 margin in 1973, many thought that it was a great day for women. The positive effects of legalizing abortion would be to uplift the dignity of women, reduce child abuse, and provide more stability to the institution of marriage. Many times we heard in the past that eliminating unwanted pregnancies would decrease divorce and allow for more stable marriages. And in the developing countries, it would have the added advantage of being an effective form of population control.

However, these promises have been proven to be false. The legalization of abortion was a boost to the sexual revolution's quest for "free love," but it has only served to turn women into objects of lust and fantasy, for there is no responsibility needed on the part of men. Therefore, divorce rates are higher than ever, marriage as an institution is hurting badly, and child abuse — of all sorts — dominates the media headlines more than ever. On every count, the false prophets of "family planning" were off the mark.

Even though many developing countries have the common sense to avoid abortion as a way of planning their families, it has a stronghold in America because people have fallen for the lies that were spread around it. So many people are so confused about the issue of abortion that they're not really interested in hearing the truth. But to understand better why abortion has become so widespread, we must try to understand these lies.

- ## LIE NO. 1: 'IT ISN'T REALLY A BABY — JUST SOME TISSUE, OR A GLOB OF CELLS'

Roe vs. Wade was only decided in 1973, and yet in that short period of time, the abortionists arranged the playing field to fit with their goals. They deceived many into thinking that the unborn infant is only a "glob of cells," and just "a piece of tissue." Many women have ended up on the operating table unaware of the intricate development going on within their body, unaware that the baby's heart starts beating 22 days after conception, and that the blood circulating through the child is its own, not the mother's. By week eight of the child's development, every organ is in place, bones begin to replace cartilage, and fingerprints begin to form. Also, the baby is beginning to hear (source: www.nrlc.org). These are all developments within the span of two months' time, well within the first trimester, when the majority of abortions take place.

- ## LIE NO. 2: PRO-LIFERS ARE DANGEROUS AND OUT TO REPRESS MY RIGHTS

The abortionists have also succeeded in distorting the views of those promoting the dignity of women, motherhood, and the right to life. They have made it almost accepted dogma that those favoring life are against women's rights and the dignity of womanhood. Those favoring life are looked on as the radical right and a dangerous group of people. This destroys all attempts at dialogue, which could go toward helping women arrive at the truth for themselves. Many have accused pro-lifers of degrading women because we do not favor abortion. Yet, it is abortion that's degrading to women.

- ## LIE NO. 3: 'I'M IN CHARGE OF MY OWN BODY, SO MY CHOICE TRUMPS ALL ELSE'

Today we often mistakenly think we have the right to do whatever we want with our bodies, as long as it doesn't hurt anyone else. First of all, abortion does hurt someone else, but second and more importantly, we actually can't do whatever we want with our bodies; they are a gift from God and belong to Him. (See 1 Corinthians 6:19-20.) We will only be truly free and fulfilled if we use our bodies to glorify God, and use them according to His plan.

- ## LIE NO. 4: 'I'M NOT HEALTHY, WEALTHY, OR WISE ENOUGH TO RAISE THIS BABY'

Often women find themselves in situations where they can't pay the bills, and have a hard time putting food on the table. In those times, for a woman having a first (or another) baby, it can seem incredibly overwhelming, leading some to seek out abortion as an alternative. However, no financial crunch can justify taking another person's life. If it's truly impossible to raise the baby due to financial problems, there is always the

11

"adoption option." There is always a way to choose life.

- **LIE NO. 5: 'MY PREGNANCY IS A MISTAKE, SO I'M NOT GOING TO HAVE THIS CHILD'**

Unfortunately, many believe that every pregnancy must be "planned," as if they had the power to make it happen themselves! God is the author of life, and only He ultimately has the power to bestow life or take it away. The idea that a child is a "mistake" because the pregnancy wasn't "planned" is not a justification for abortion. No human life is an accident. Every human life deserves to be treated with dignity, respect, and honor. An "unwanted" pregnancy can become viewed by some as a disease that can be cured by a "simple and painless procedure." Clearly, this is a terrible way of thinking.

- **LIE NO. 6: 'MY HUSBAND / BOYFRIEND / FAMILY MEMBERS SAY I HAVE TO GET AN ABORTION'**

Often the family and significant others aren't supportive in choosing life. To family members, abortion can seem like a good option to help avoid embarrassment or financial burdens. Also many husbands and boyfriends sadly view abortion as a form of contraception. This further degrades women as they are often seen as nothing more than sex objects. Abortion has therefore lessened the need for male responsibility, and the sexual act carries no commitment as pregnancy can always be ended through abortion. This kind of pressure on the pregnant woman is the furthest thing from loving her; it's just doing what is easiest for themselves, instead of doing what is best for her.

• LIE NO. 7: 'ABORTION IS NOT A BIG PROBLEM'

A statistic largely ignored by mainstream society: There are over 1.2 million infants killed yearly in this country through abortion, and nearly 60 million worldwide. And this is being done in virtually complete anonymity! The number of 1.2 million in this country alone, contrasts with the 58,000 U.S. serviceman killed in the entire Vietnam War, and the nearly 3,000 killed in the terrorists' attack on American soil on September 11, 2001. Yet how could this staggering number of unborn dying yearly go unnoticed and happen in such a short time? The supporters of abortion would have us believe that abortion is a "private matter" and "the best thing to do." They would argue that the "right to life, liberty, and the pursuit of happiness" found in the United States Constitution do not apply to the unborn human.

Mother Teresa once said, "America needs no words from me to see how your decision in *Roe vs. Wade* has deformed a great nation. The so-called right to abortion has pitted mothers against their children and women against men. It has portrayed the greatest of gifts — a child — as a competitor, an intrusion, and an inconvenience" (Mother Teresa — "Notable and Quotable," *Wall Street Journal,* Feb. 25, 1994, p. A14).

Abortion is a huge lie, and many have fallen for the idea that it's an acceptable option for families. In order to achieve healing from the effects of abortion, the lies of abortion must be exposed for what they are, so the truth can come forth. Only in the context of truth can true healing be attained, healing for those directly involved with abortion, those indirectly involved, and for the whole world — since abortion affects all of us, one way or another.

This booklet is an effort to help the people who have been involved with abortion come to grips with the truth, so they can move into the realm of healing. The co-authors of this booklet both travel the country speaking to people about the mercy of God and the sanctity and gift of all human life. In doing so, they have found that the work of spreading the truth and assisting people with their healing is the only way to reform America, which has been deformed by the lies of abortion.

CHAPTER 2
Effects of Abortion on the Mother
Post-Abortion Syndrome

THE DETRIMENTAL EFFECTS

A constellation of symptoms has been identified which bears striking resemblance to the symptoms of "Post-traumatic stress disorder." When the stressor is abortion, this disorder bears the name "Post-abortion syndrome."

Although the medical community at large does not formally recognize the syndrome, the experience of women is clear. Some of the emotional symptoms noted by women include lowered self-esteem, fear of pregnancy, psychological numbing, and an inability to process their anger, sadness, and guilt. Behavioral manifestations include eating and sleep disorders, promiscuity, substance abuse, and sexual dysfunction. Medical complications include sterility, miscarriages, tubal pregnancy, and an increased risk of breast cancer. Spiritually, many women find it difficult to accept God's forgiveness. The persistent sadness about the death of a child is often exacerbated at events like baptism, graduation, and Mother's Day celebrations. Anniversary reactions are also common. (The book *Detrimental Effects of Abortion*, published in 2001 by Thomas Strahan, is an excellent overview of the many studies on post-abortion aftermath that have been completed to date.)

Another study, *Women's Health after Abortion*, published in 2002 by the DeVeber Institute is also a good source for facts about the effects of abortion on women, both physically and psychologically. The authors of this book state, in their conclusion,

> The difficulties of measuring the physical consequences of abortion are legion. ... To begin with, a significant proportion of women simply refuse to be interviewed about their experience. Much more work needs to be done, but already we know that women who have an abortion are much likelier to commit suicide than women who deliver their babies. We also know that women often feel ambivalent about their decision to abort. When offered supportive counseling, as they are in Sweden, they are more likely not to abort. In many instances, abortion, far from being a woman's free choice, is the product of coercive pressure from her male partner or family. It is also known that abortion is often not a good solution for women who have a psychiatric history, live in abusive relationships, believe abortion is morally wrong, or are adolescents. Abortion deepens the tribulation of these women (p. 279).

CHILD ABUSE

The notion was proposed that child abuse would decline in countries where abortion was legalized, as many believed that the abused child was one that was unwanted at birth. Terminating the pregnancy would be doing the unborn a "service" by not bringing them into a society where they might suffer injury and not be loved. Unfortunately, scientific studies have shown that child abuse has increased dramatically since the legalization of abortion, perhaps related to the lessened dignity of women and their inability to deal with stress. Dr. P. Ney wrote in the *Canada Journal of Psychiatry*, "Recent evidence indicates that women harbor strong guilt feelings long after their abortions. Guilt is one important cause of child battering and infanticide. Abortion lowers women's self esteem and there are studies reporting a major loss of self-esteem in battering parents …" (*Can Jnl. Psych*, Vol. 32, pp. 610-620).

TESTIMONIES ARE TELLING

The best way to understand the damage done by abortion is to listen to the testimonies of those who suffer that damage. Two such testimonies follow. (A very large collection can be found at www.priestsforlife.org.) The stories that follow are different, but they share a common thread, one common to all women who have had an abortion.

Although researchers have been studying the negative effects of abortion for decades, the research done so far has not been as comprehensive as it needs to be. There is no doubt that abortion harms women, and testimonies from women like those at the website just mentioned are constantly collected by pro-life ministries. Yet when supporters of abortion claim that only a small percentage of women suffer after abortion, one must keep in mind that there is no basis for saying that the percentage is small. What is needed is research far more comprehensive than what has been done to date. Only then will anyone be able to speak with any certitude about the magnitude of the damage.

CHAPTER 3
Laura's Story

I am so happy to share my witness regarding abortion, and how it has affected my life. It's a wonderful opportunity to keep alive the memory of my own three aborted children. The following testimony is the often-overlooked result of my fall from chastity. It is the quiet, unknown factor that is often ignored with regard to the battle for life.

As I look back at what happened in my life, let me start with an unusual entry in the *Diary of Saint Maria Faustina*. Saint Faustina wrote that she was seized with violent pains. She convulsed with pain for three hours. No medicine had any effect on her. Jesus helped her realize that she had taken part in His Agony in the Garden, and that in this way she took part in these sufferings in order to offer reparation to God for the souls murdered in the wombs of "wicked mothers." She went through these sufferings three times.

Her doctors could not get to the bottom of it, and no medicine could lessen the sufferings. She told the doctor that never before in her life had she experienced such sufferings. The doctor declared he did not know what sort of pains they were. Saint Faustina understood the nature of the pains, because the Lord Himself made them known to her. She wrote, "Yet, when I think that I may perhaps suffer in this way again, I tremble. But I don't know whether I'll ever again suffer in this way; I leave that to God. What pleases God to send, I will accept with submission and love. If only I could save even one soul from murder by means of these sufferings" (#1276).

FORGIVING SELF

For decades, I saw myself as one of the "wicked mothers" of whom she spoke. I was unable to forgive myself for what I had done. Reading this particular paragraph brought back memories of past choices I had made. These choices are extremely difficult to think about. I reflect back on my three abortions, and I never knew the future effects my abortions would have, on myself — and others. We begin to realize that not only have we denied ourselves personally the joy of God's children, but even those within the framework of our own families have been denied the opportunity of experiencing the valuable roles that God intended for them. The knowledge, which never leaves you as a parent, is that you have the blood of your children on your hands. There is a perpetual void that can only be filled by the infinite mercy of our Lord.

In 1975, my first unborn child was conceived out of wedlock. I was 20 years old, single, and in the Army. I was very much separated from God and the Church. I was in love with the father, but because we were states apart, I did not tell him about the pregnancy until after the abortion. I was quite young, independent, and naive. I trusted my job superior who was also my Commanding Officer. When I told him that I was pregnant, he quickly lined up a doctor's visit for me, as he put it, "to take care of things." Little did I know what was happening the day of that "visit," nor did I know what the word "abortion" even meant. Though under heavy sedation, I woke up briefly during the procedure as the doctors were examining the baby's body parts. "Hey Joe, this was a boy — look here."

I did not know, at that point in my life, that a mother could murder her child. Point blank! My life was not sheltered, but I simply had never heard of such a thing, nor did I know that it was possible, nor that it was a possibility that such a thing could be committed! Does that make sense? *Roe vs. Wade* was decided about two years prior to my abortion, and I had never even heard about the case. I turned to my Commanding Officer, whom I trusted, as a leader and a helping hand. I worked at an annex of the Pentagon at that time, and he sent me to my "visit" at Walter Reed Hospital.

I thought that I was going in for a "check up." No one sat down and talked with me, or advised me about what was going to happen. No one explained that what was about to take place might alter my life for decades in ways that can never easily be described. I was drugged. My child was aborted, and afterwards I had to drive myself home — about 20 miles away. I was so heavily sedated, it's a wonder I made it home alive. I was running off the road repeatedly, while trying to stop the blood flow at the same time — what a horrible memory. After the medications subsided, I understood what had just happened to me, and what I had just done. I was numb.

I remember sadly telling the father afterwards what I had done to our child. To this day, I can still I hear him quietly telling me that he would have loved the child as much as he loved me. He asked me how I could have done this to him without his consent. We have not kept in touch. If I saw him again, I thought, for only a minute, I would like to be able to ask for forgiveness from him. This memory haunted me for decades and yet seems like only yesterday.

MONEY PROBLEMS

Three years later, I found myself pregnant again. This time the abortion was out of convenience and fear. How would it look? Not yet married and my husband-to-be was the father. We had little money or income, and we knew that this "quick fix" for the unexpected pregnancy would keep us from getting into debt. We just couldn't afford a baby quite yet. My husband-to-be took me to the abortion clinic.

For years later, I spent many a drunken night covering up the silent pain in my heart. I was grieving and didn't really know why.

Soon after our marriage, my husband and I aborted our second child. God had blessed us with a second child, but we still didn't feel we were ready. Looking back, I see that another little angel was wiped from the face of the earth. What were we thinking? Where were our lives headed? We had both bought into the lie of our culture … "tissue, blob of flesh, etc." A friend escorted me to the abortion mill, and another one of our children was destroyed, never to know the love of its mother and father. How could we have allowed this to happen?

MERCIFUL TRUTH

My aborted children remind me of the Prayer of St. Francis that states "Where there is error, let me bring truth." As a convert to Catholicism, these "truths" of my personal offenses to God and my children had to be painfully faced once I returned back to the Catholic Church that I had deserted as a teenager. The reality of our sinful offenses as parents was even more amplified when my husband also became a Catholic.

There is a denial factor that can begin to take over. It is a very hard thing to admit to what you have done — once, twice, however many times. We don't understand God's mercy so we can't face the sin — whatever the degree. Before the sin, we can't face the problem because we don't know His love and don't trust Him. Then, after the sin, we tend to deny what we have done. The truth is, we can be bathed in His mercy. He who is all good can — and wants — to heal us completely. Were it not for the message of the Divine Mercy, my husband and I would never have been able to reach the point in our lives where we are now: "at peace with the pain." Without the promise of God's mercy, we could not bear the pain from our own pierced hearts.

My husband and I have been married now for 24 years. I have great love for him. He has been a wonderful father and provider. As I proudly watch our two precious, living children exercise their adulthood at 19 and 21, I am frequently reminded of my other three that are not with us. I have accepted the reality that I have five beloved children. I live one day at a time with loving trust, total surrender, and cheerfulness as lived by the Holy Family at Nazareth. These are the spiritual salves from the Great Physician that cover my woundedness. God is so merciful to me in being so forgiving.

SURPRISE CALL

Our diocese recently held its first Rachel's Vineyard Retreat in October 2002. These are weekend retreats for women who have had abortions and want to receive healing. This weekend retreat began on the eve of St. Faustina's Feast Day (October 5), and was very emotionally and spiritually healing for me. Most amazing, the following transpired a few months later:

One week before Christmas 2002, I received a phone call from a man I had not spoken with for 14 years. He was the father of my first unborn child — the one from whom I had longed to ask forgiveness. A most unusual turn of events for him was a long overdue healing for me. Charlie's sales associate had just been fired, and he had immediately been assigned to take over a delivery route which lead him hundreds of miles from his home, and down a busy highway that passed right by the front door of my workplace. He called and asked me if we could meet "if only for a few minutes." In my heart, I knew that this was the once in a lifetime opportunity for which I had often prayed. However, I also knew that without my husband's knowledge or consent, I would not allow one moment of the removal of this cross that I had learned to live with. I turned all of my fears and concerns over to The Divine Mercy, trusting only in Him. I asked Jesus to give me the courage to talk with my husband about the phone call. How good God is, to have given me a spouse with such a kind, trusting, and loving heart!

I agreed to meet Charlie in a Catholic

Church at 3 p.m., the Hour of Great Mercy; it seemed only right to be in front of Our Lord in the tabernacle during that hour. We went into the church and sat in the crying room. In my pocket, was a portion of the witness I had written for this booklet. I unfolded the paragraph that was written about our child and asked him to read it. With tears in his eyes, Charlie asked me what I wanted from him. My answer was forgiveness for having aborted our child. Looking me straight in the eyes, he responded, "Laura, I forgave you 28 years ago!" Whoever would have thought? I never would have known this had I not been given this moment in time.

I found out that in 1995 (the same year I had returned to the Catholic Church), Charlie had been in a terrible car collision. A drunk driver was trying to commit suicide and hit him head-on at a very high speed. He told me that he had to survive after that accident because he had some "unfinished business to attend to." That business was to see me again. Charlie could have been killed, and I would never have been able to hear those sweet words of forgiveness that helped heal me in a way that I would have never expected. It never occurred to me, until writing my witness for this booklet, that Charlie's initials are CDM, which for me represents the Chaplet of Divine Mercy. Lord, how good You are to me!

I would be remiss if I did not add the fact that I have completely forgiven — from the deepest parts of my heart — all the people in my life that in any way played a part in my abortions. I am certain that they never could have imagined how their actions helped cause such havoc in my life. I am also convinced that if they had known the long-term effects of what they were doing, they never would have assisted in the first place. I give back to them the mercy and love that our Lord has first given me. We know not what we do … .

My hope is that those reading this booklet will reflect on the words of Mother Teresa of Calcutta, "It is a very great poverty to decide that a child must die that you might live as you wish."

CHAPTER 4
Joan's Story

At the root of my two abortions, I know now was the tragic destruction within our family. My father was a violent alcoholic. Our home was filled with fear and chaos: We walked on eggshells waiting for the next terrifying round of violence. Alcohol abuse and adultery surrounded us, and there was also physical, emotional, and sexual abuse.

CHALLENGING PAST

We lived in a nice neighborhood where families were close. My father was publicly carrying on a very scandalous affair and everyone in the neighborhood knew about it. The gossip mill was constantly churning out all the latest sordid details of their relationship. Our young minds were filled with trash. All trust and dignity were violated both in and out of the home. It seemed as if every trace of innocence was completely destroyed. My mother survived the constant humiliation and fear by medicating herself with tranquilizers and alcohol. It was a home without love, and I do not remember a single hug from either parent. The first recollection I have of my mom telling me she loved me was when I was 30 years old. We received a Catholic education during the day, and at night and on the weekends, we lived in fear and violence. Looking back, I remember thinking, "Where are You, God?" It seemed no religion could save us.

As a teenager, I desperately searched for love and acceptance. Learning from my experiences at home, I continued the familiar pattern of abusive relationships. I fell away from the Church and got pregnant in high school to escape my life at home. I wanted the baby very much because I wanted to know what it would feel like to be loved unconditionally. My son, William, was born in my senior year of high school. I married the father, but left him when William was two, for fear of my child's safety. Barely present as a father, my husband took no interest in our child, provided no financial support, and his womanizing, as well as drug and alcohol addictions, were constantly putting William and me in danger.

WEALTHY SECOND HUSBAND

I eventually got engaged to a wealthy man and during the engagement found myself pregnant again. This man prided himself on his high position within the community and was very embarrassed by the pregnancy. Under extreme duress and with a looming medical question as to whether or not the pregnancy was viable, I was set up for what the doctors called, a "therapeutic abortion." My fiancée would not be seen at the hospital, and in the final moments just before the procedure, the doctor said it appeared that everything was normal. He asked me if I still wanted to go through with the procedure. Tragically, I went ahead with the abortion because I was afraid that my living son, William, would lose this second chance of having a father and a stable home life.

At the time of the abortion in the 1970s, I knew nothing about saline abortions, and the doctor did not provide me with any medical facts about the nature of the procedure or photos of the development of the child in utero. I had just turned 20, and had never seen a single gestational photo or had any idea what a fetus was capable of, or how formed it was, at any given stage. I had bought into the pro-abortion lie that these abortion doctors were not killing babies; no, they were just removing unformed pieces of tissue.

EXPERIENCING THE LOSS

After the injection, I felt a thrashing around inside me. I asked the nurse what was going on, and she said, "Nothing, it is just the medication." I felt something snap. My mind was reeling when I felt the sheer size and weight of what I was delivering. I heard a loud, heavy "plunk" fall into something steely and cold that was placed under me. Why was it so heavy and large? I asked myself. "What was that?" I asked the nurse. She replied, "It's a boy." How could she know it's a boy? My mind raced. I was frantic. I started to look and heard interiorly a gentle, kind voice say, "Don't look." Later, I would find out my son's tomb was a stainless steel bedpan.

My fiancée and I went ahead with the wedding, and once again, I found myself in a very abusive marriage. The second abortion, a first trimester dilation and curettage abortion (D&C), came at the end of that second marriage. It just seemed I did not know how to be part of, or how to nurture any healthy relationships in my life. The primary thought I had at the time was survival, as I was about to be a single parent again in my early 20s. The pattern of abusive men continued into my mid-30s. After many incidences of violence and rape, in desperation, I finally cried out to God to help me: Send me a man who is kind and true. Three months after that prayer, He sent me my husband. Realizing I had been given a great gift, I began my journey back to the Catholic Church. My husband's conversion to the faith followed closely thereafter.

SEEING IT IN A NEW LIGHT

One year into our marriage, at age 38, and 18 years after the saline abortion that viciously took the life of my son, Matthew, I saw a photo of a saline aborted child for the first time. That is when I found out what the nurse had seen, and how that gentle voice was actually protecting me. Matthew, like the child I saw in the picture, was a perfectly formed five-month-old baby. I screamed, then sobbed. I was shocked to see a beautiful child whose body had been charred and blackened. I now know the thrashing I felt was my son moving around, convulsing in pain as his little body was being burned alive by the saline solution. He was gasping as he was drowning in that poisonous solution.

It is difficult not to remember my aborted children every time I look at my living son, as I can see the scars of my two abortions on his face. I can see the disappointment of the family that never was, the encouragement and the joy his brothers would have surely been in his life. When I look into the beautiful, trusting eyes of my six-year-old granddaughter, I sometimes ponder: how many other grandchildren would there have been? The sin of abortion is so grievous that my mind cannot grasp the loss, and only my heart can bear witness to the gravity of the sin. Only a loving Savior can make it bearable.

COMFORT IN THE CHAPLET

I used to feel abortion was the unforgivable sin. Praying the words of the Chaplet of Divine Mercy for the first time offered the greatest source of help in dealing with overwhelming feelings of condemnation. Repetition of the prayer brought all of Sacred Scripture's promises to life. My eyes were opened that Jesus' sacrifice was complete, the atonement that His Father could not refuse. I came to see that resurrection life was for all His children. It is the prize the Cross had bought for every one of us! For the first time, I knew my children were in heaven, and that I was forgiven by the grace of a merciful Savior.

However, I still experience deep sorrow over the remaining effects of the sins. I realize the eternal difference my two aborted sons, Matthew and Jonathan, would have made on this earth. All too late, I now completely understand that they were created for a unique purpose. They number among countless souls that would have touched others and reaped a harvest for the kingdom. My heart will always weep over them. My heart knows them and I miss them. The world lost the God-given gifts they were meant to share on this earth and the difference their lives would have made. Until I hold them and see them, I join my tears to those of Our Sorrowful Mother's, and I place all my hope and need for comfort in The Divine Mercy.

The witness of these two women speak to the horrors of abortion. The physical, psychological, and spiritual aftereffects of abortion are many and varied. It is as if the words of Jeremiah found in Sacred Scripture manifest as emotional, bodily, and psychological symptoms; *"Rachel mourns her children, she refuses to be consoled because her children are no more"* (Jeremiah 31:15, NAB).

CHAPTER 5
Effects of Abortion on Others Involved

It Doesn't Just Affect the Mother

Doctor David Reardon wrote "Forgotten Fathers and Their Unforgettable Children," (*The Post Abortion Review*, p.4, Fall 1996). He commented on the work of sociologist Arthur Shostak, who in the early '70s, accompanied his girlfriend to an abortion clinic. By the time the abortion was done, Shostak was shocked at how troubled he had become. For the next 10 years, he studied 1,000 men who accompanied their wives or girlfriends to an abortion clinic. The study was published in *Men and Abortion: Lessons, Losses, and Love* (Praeger, 1984).

Shostak found that the majority of men surveyed felt isolated and angry with themselves, and were concerned about what effects the procedure would have on their partner. The study found that abortion is far more stressful on men than most people would believe. More than 80 percent said they had begun to think about the child that might have been born, and 29 percent said that they fantasized frequently about the child. Shostak reported that many men cried during the interview. Nearly half had urged the woman to choose an abortion, and an overwhelming majority opposed any legal restrictions on abortion.

Researcher Emily Miller studied over 400 couples with women who had had an abortion; she found that 70 percent of the relationships ended within one month of the procedure. Sociologist A. Shostak found that 75 percent of male respondents had persistent day and night dreams about the "child that never was." And Linda B. Franke wrote, "In my research, almost every relationship between single people broke up either before or after the abortion" (www.RoevWade.org).

In addition, Shostak reported that men feel the need to work through their pain and guilt privately, and that the male does not share his pain with his pastor or even a close male companion. And in another study, two-thirds of men reported feelings of guilt, compared to 56 percent of women. And over one-third said they regretted the choice made compared to one-quarter of women.

REWRITING MASCULINITY

Men have also reported a number of problems that they felt were related to the abortion. These include broken relationships, sexual dysfunction, substance abuse, grief, depression, and feelings of helplessness, guilt, and even suicidal behavior. Dr. Vincent Rue, a psychologist with extensive study in the area of post-abortion issues, said that:

> Induced abortion reinforces defective problem solving on the part of the male by encouraging detachment, desertion, and irresponsibility. ... Abortion rewrites the rule of masculinity. While a male is expected to be strong, abortion makes him feel weak. A male is

expected to be responsible, yet abortion encourages him to act without concern for the innocent and to destroy any identifiable and undesirable outcomes of his sexual decision-making and/or attachments. ... Whether or not the male was involved in the abortion decision, his inability to function in a socially prescribed manner (i.e., to protect and provide) leaves him wounded and confused (Vincent Rue, "The Effects of Abortion on Men," *Ethics and Medics* 21 [4]:3-4, 1996).

Some family therapists suggest an abortion may create an unsettling ambiguity in the "family boundary." For example, every time post-abortive mothers or fathers are asked how many children they have, do they count the aborted child as their offspring?

'SURVIVING' CHILDREN AFFECTED

The work of Dr. Philip Ney, a Canadian psychiatrist, and his wife, Marie, have uncovered another fascinating dimension of the damage done by abortion: namely, its effect on the children who are not aborted. What does it do to a child's psyche to realize that her own mother could have legally killed her? How is a child's behavior shaped when he understands that he is alive because he is "wanted," and fears that he can still be killed if he is no longer wanted tomorrow? What is it like for a child to have brothers or sisters who were aborted? The study of these questions has led to the discovery of "Post-abortion Survivor Syndrome."

According to the study done by Ring-Cassidy and Gentles, in *Women's Health after Abortion*, "Post-abortal women report that their ability to respond to the remaining or future child(ren) can be manifested in several ways: a feeling of emotional numbness which leads to a lack of bonding, acting out of hostility and anger which can result in child abuse, and considering future children as 'replacement children' who become overindulged" (p. 227).

There are at least 10 different types of abortion survivors. These children experience "survivor guilt" and "existential anxiety." Their world is on an uncertain foundation. They feel guilty for being the ones selected to live. They may feel guilty for less than perfect behavior that they perceive resulted in the parents choosing abortion over life. These and other symptoms are a major obstacle to evangelizing the young. The Gospel of a loving and forgiving God is all the more foreign, yet all the more needed, by a generation that has been taught the laws and mores of a culture of death: that they are disposable at someone else's choice. In short, the wounds of abortion are carried from one generation to the next and affect everyone in those generations.

ERIC'S STORY

Eric Eckenrode is an inspirational singer and speaker who shares about the pain of abortion from a father's perspective. Learn more about his music and ministry at www.vaughaneckenrode.com. He recounted his story for us:

AN APPOINTMENT AT THE CLINIC

My day began as usual at six in the morning — hitting the weights at the gym where I also worked as a personal trainer during my teenage years. The only difference about that day was that I was in a hurry. I needed to pick up my girlfriend, so we would be on time for our appointment at an abortion clinic.

I was annoyed and aggravated as I shared with my training partner that I was unsure if I would be able to make our second workout of the day — at five that afternoon — because of my girlfriend's scheduled abortion. We quickly finished our workout, and I was on my way to pick her up.

She had professed her love for me, and I repaid her by getting her pregnant. When she told me that she was expecting, we talked it over. With the encouragement of a school guidance counselor, we agreed to abort our child. We didn't dare tell our parents, and we didn't need to anyway, for there was, and still is, no parental consent law.

SECOND THOUGHTS

As we drove to meet our appointment, I noticed that she was sad and distant, but I didn't care. I was focused on getting back to the gym on time. Once inside the clinic, thinking she was in good hands with all the professional-looking people in white coats, I found myself a seat and waited. Meanwhile, she filled out the papers and then sat next to me and also waited. We received no counseling, advice, or suggestion about the gravity of our decision. When they called her name after many hours, she looked at me and said words that I will never forget: "I don't want to do this."

I turned to her and said, "We've already talked about it. You've got to do this. Go!" I was relieved, thinking this would soon be over. She looked at me in disappointment, then turned away, and followed the nurse. When she finally came out, I paid the $160 charge, took her home, and then rushed to the gym, where it turned out I was only a few minutes late. We never talked about that day again.

YOUNGER YEARS

What had led me to this moment? Let me tell you how I grew up.

I am the youngest of three boys. My parents divorced, and my mother raised us boys without support from our father. My older brothers defined my world. They represented the living embodiment of what it meant to be a man. As I grew up, I knew I needed to look like a man, act like a man, and talk like a man.

So I began bodybuilding at the tender age of 11. In no time at all, I found myself consumed with the sport. I set my sights on becoming "Mr. America." I entered my first competitive bodybuilding contest when I was just 15 years old. I took first place. Winning boosted my confidence in the sport but blinded me from being able to look outside of myself, leading to the abortion decision.

PRO BODYBUILDER

For the next 12 years after the abortion, I followed my dream of becoming a professional bodybuilder. I made it into the muscle magazines. I took the "Mr. North America Middle Weight Title" in 1991, moved to Las Vegas, and lived the life. Tragically, the height of my success as a bodybuilder indicated the abyss of my spiritual state.

I maintained my body on steroids, synthetic hormones, and painkillers. I suffocated my spirit on cocaine and amphetamines. At my lowest point, I experienced rebirth. I was staying with a friend, and we talked about my life. I announced, proudly, that I was the Devil's right-hand man and that I had no soul. Inspired by the Holy Spirit, He suggested to me that I need do nothing more than ask what I felt in my heart and keep my mind open.

That following evening, as I prepared to lie down and find sleep, I found, instead, the strength and the will to ask. I kept my heart and mind open, just as my friend had suggested.

Then I found myself on my knees in prayer for the first time. God's love filled my body, my heart, my mind, and my soul.

FINDING CHRIST

I had sought God and had found Jesus Christ. His Sorrowful Passion went through me, and I wept like a little child. When I encountered Jesus, I asked Him, "Why now, after all the crazy things in my life, why are You here?" He responded, "I have always been with you. But you have never listened. I have spoken to your heart always."

More personal struggles followed that initial moment of grace until I finally gave up drugs for good. Then, at 29, I went to confession and received my First Holy Communion. A year later, I was confirmed. The dedication and perseverance I had applied to the goals of obtaining optimal gains in bodybuilding, I now apply to my Catholic faith, including the Holy Eucharist and confession, personal prayer, and devotions like the Rosary and the Chaplet of Divine Mercy.

Then, in 1998, I attended my first pro-life march in Washington, DC. As I looked around and saw all the pictures of the aborted babies, the reality of my baby's death finally struck home. I began to cry and found that I could not stop. One of the gifts God has given me is putting my prayers in song. So, as I continued to sort through my strong emotions, I knew I had to write a song about my experience. After much prayer and struggle, I wrote a song called "My Plea — Let the Healing Begin." I dedicated it to the memory of my son, Vaughan.

PROJECT RACHEL

God always knows what I need and supplies me with wonderful and talented people to help spread His message. One such person was the former coordinator of Project Rachel in Washington, DC, Maureen Breitenbach. Her words to me upon listening for the first time to "My Plea — Let the Healing Begin" were: "I'm so sorry to hear about the loss of your child." She helped me grieve my loss.

Maureen also inspired me to write a song to the mother of my child with whom I have lost contact. I called it "Apology," and I pray that she will hear this song someday. I've come to realize, through my meeting with Christ and His Church, God's mercy is great enough to provide healing for all wounds, even those suffering the trauma of an abortion, which is called "Post-Abortive Stress" (PAS).

I now work with Project Rachel where my songs have been effective in spreading the message of forgiveness and healing. We visit schools, campuses, and parishes throughout the country to talk about the reality of the pain of abortion and the healing power of God. I share about that pain from a father's perspective.

And God in His mercy called me to start a family — this time, the right way. On June 8, 2002, the Feast of the Immaculate Heart of Mary, I married a beautiful, inspiring woman named Nicole. And we were blessed quickly with the gift of new life. Three months into our pregnancy, we had a 4-D sonogram done, which shows clearly our tiny and fully formed human son, Joseph Benjamin. Our baby was born in spring of 2003.

Jesus has once again proved to me that He is The Divine Mercy — that He will always love even the greatest sinner who turns towards Him. "Jesus, I trust in You!" (This testimony was first published in *Marian Helper* magazine, Spring 2003.)

CHAPTER 6
Obstacles to Healing and Overcoming Them

CAN I BE FORGIVEN?

Unfortunately, many go through life believing that God could never forgive them of anything, let alone a serious sin. Perhaps some were raised to believe that the God of Justice is lurking around every corner, waiting for them to sin, so that He can condemn them to hell. And like the fictional God that they have created, they too reject others and themselves for not being perfect.

And yet, God's love and mercy is unfathomable, and no human mind will ever understand it. That is the beauty of the Lord and His Divine Mercy, and why this message needs to be told! The God we know is a God of love and mercy, and His love is never ending! This does not mean we can do whatever we want, or that we should not strive for perfection. However, it does mean that we should always try to love God and neighbor, and when we fall short of the mark, we should go back to Him in humility and ask for forgiveness. We must believe that God forgives! We also need to forgive others, and especially ourselves. St. Faustina wrote, "We resemble God most when we forgive our neighbor" (*Diary*, 1148). However, that also means forgiveness of self! I doubt that we really can forgive others, and especially ourselves, unless we first accept God's forgiveness. Do you really believe that God could forgive YOU for such a sin?

Two Facets of Healing

There are two facets of healing, including post-abortion healing. One involves knowing that God forgives you; He died for you and His blood delivers you from all your guilt. The other is, knowing that as God forgives you, you are made clean, and you do not need to walk around wearing a cloak of shame.

The *Catechism of the Catholic Church* teaches us in paragraph 1443:

> During His public life, Jesus not only forgave sins, but also made plain the effect of this forgiveness: He reintegrated forgiven sinners into the community of the People of God from which sin had alienated or even excluded them. A remarkable sign of this is the fact that Jesus receives sinners at His table, a gesture that expresses in an astonishing way both God's forgiveness and the return to the bosom of the People of God.

Recently, one of the authors (BT) got into an argument with a friend, and for a period of time, she withdrew her love and did not speak to him. Most of us tend to pull back and withdraw love when we are angry. As we travel and speak on Divine Mercy and the gift of life, we hear many stories of family members not communicating with each other because of a disagreement of many years ago. But God does not withdraw His love when we sin, so why should we withdraw our love to others and ourselves? We know that God hates the sin, but we doubt that He loves the sinner: we forget that His love is unconditional. In spite of our sinfulness, we are all sons and daughters of God! *"For God has consigned all men to disobedience, that He may have mercy upon all"* (Rom 10:32).

DEALING WITH THE GRIEF

There is a difference between guilt and shame. Guilt is, "I did evil." Shame is, "I am evil." Certainly guilt is useful if not taken to extremes. Even if the person has worked through the forgiveness issue, one still must deal with the grief of the death of a loved one. In most cultures, there is a ceremony at the time of death of a loved one, and it assists the family in dealing with their grief. However, this is not the case in abortion, so at the death of the child, there is no chance for closure. Grief is normal and part of the healing process, but carried to excess, it can be crippling. Why are we so tough on others and ourselves when we stumble? Laura and Joan grieve daily over the loss of their children, and Joan in particular finds Mother's Day difficult.

Shame causes us to believe that we are bad because we have done a bad thing. Shame allows us to keep beating ourselves up; to keep going over and over in our minds, things like, "Why did I do this?" and "How could I have done such a thing?" and "What a worthless person I am!"

All the shame and self-doubt enters our mind over and over and over, and we become so deeply troubled that we wonder if God could ever forgive such a miserable soul. Yet, the God of Mercy is ready to forgive and show us mercy. We can find comfort in the words Our Lord spoke to St. Faustina, **"The greater the sinner, the greater the right he has to My mercy"** (*Diary*, 723). Committing a terrible sin does not make us bad people. In fact, many support group meetings, such as Alcoholics Anonymous, include phrases in the meeting like, "Hi, I'm so and so. I am an alcoholic. I have done bad things, but I am not a bad person." And one of the fruits of those meetings is acceptance, a feeling that "maybe I am not so bad after all. Maybe I can overcome my problem." And isn't that what Jesus tried to do, to bring the sinners back into the community of God?

LIMITLESS FORGIVENESS

How many times has God forgiven us? God is always there, ready to forgive, and there are no limits to His mercy! Our Lord told St. Faustina, **"Apostle of My mercy, proclaim to the whole world My unfathomable mercy"** (*Diary*, 1142). His mercy is so great that we will never be able to comprehend it. It is like an ocean that has no bottom. All we have to do is trust in Him and float in the great ocean of mercy. And in the calm of the water, we must try to forgive ourselves, and others, becoming an icon of Jesus reflected off the glassy, flat surface of the unfathomable ocean of mercy.

Think about how many times we pray the Our Father, *"And forgive us our debts, as we also have forgiven our debtors"* (Mt 6:12). We are living in a time of great mercy, and yet the outpouring of God's mercy cannot be received as long as we have not forgiven those who have offended us. How can we love the God we cannot see, if we cannot love the brother or sister we can see? In refusing to forgive our brothers and sisters, our hearts are closed and the hardness of our hearts makes us impervious to the Father's merciful love. But in confessing our sins, our hearts are opened to His grace. (See *Catechism of the Catholic Church*, 2840.)

PRODIGAL SONS AND DAUGHTERS

Reflect on the story of the Prodigal Son. The father had to let the son go and make his own choices, even though he knew that they were bad ones. After the son had squandered all his inheritance and had no food, he returned to the father and asked for forgiveness. And Scripture says, *"But while he was yet at a distance, his father saw him and had compassion"* (Lk 15:20). Doesn't sin put all of us at a distance from God? And yet the father embraced him and rejoiced, and even had the fatted calf slaughtered! In some ways, the prodigal son experienced the kingdom of heaven on earth. He felt the unfathomable love and mercy of the Father through the compassion of his earthly father. And perhaps that is why some of us can't forgive ourselves; we have never felt the unconditional love and mercy of God from our parents.

Pope John Paul II wrote about the story of the prodigal son in his encyclical letter, *Rich in Mercy,*

The father of the prodigal son is faithful to his fatherhood, faithful to the love that he had always lavished on his son. This fidelity is expressed in the parable not only by his immediate readiness to welcome him home when he returns after having squandered his inheritance. It is expressed even more fully by that joy, that merrymaking for the squanderer after his return, merrymaking which is so generous that it provokes the opposition and hatred of the elder brother, who had never gone far away from his father and had never abandoned the home (6.1).

Many struggle more with forgiveness of self than with forgiveness of others. For many, forgiveness of self is the hardest thing to do. Yet, we were not made perfect, and we will never reach perfection this side of the grave. We learn through experience, by trial and error. Mistakes will happen, and we need to grow and learn from them. Isn't that really what living is all about?

There are those who believe that God loves them only when they do good, and could never love them when they make mistakes. Do you know someone who struggles with a low self-image? It seems no matter what they do, it is never good enough. One wonders if all the times we have been told to "do your best," or "next time you'll win!" get misunderstood and misinterpreted to mean, "You didn't win because you are no good!" Or was it perhaps an athletic coach who only praised the winners, or the teachers who commended only the honor students? For many, we buy into the mistaken notion that we are loved only when we do right or are the perfect child, and the love is withdrawn when we fall or don't excel. God's love, however, is unconditional.

UNLOADING THE GUILT

Several years ago a 75-year-old patient of mine told me (BT) the following story one day in my office. As the tears began streaming down her face, she said, "Doctor, I have never told this story to anyone. Sixty years ago, when I was just 15, I got pregnant by my future husband. I was scared and had an abortion. I never told anyone, not even him. Do you think God could ever forgive me?" She had carried all that guilt and shame for 60 years, wondering if she could ever be forgiven by the God of love and mercy!

Think of the millions of addicts who use drugs, alcohol, sex, workaholism, overeating, gambling, and other outlets and live in a world of isolation, shame, and despair. Yet, even souls striving for sanctity stumble and fall, and like the prodigal son, all must come back to the God of Mercy. Jesus spoke to St. Faustina regarding a soul striving after perfection:

> "You see, My child, what you are of yourself. The cause of your falls is that you rely

51

too much upon yourself and too little on Me. But let this not sadden you so much. You are dealing with the God of mercy, which your misery cannot exhaust. Remember, I did not allot a certain number of pardons. And the soul replied, 'Yes, I know all that, but great temptations assail me, and various doubts awaken within me and, moreover, everything irritates and discourages me.' And Jesus replied, My child, know that the greatest obstacles to holiness are discouragement and an exaggerated anxiety. These will deprive you of the ability to practice virtue. All temptations united together ought not disturb your inner peace, not even momentarily. Sensitiveness and discouragement are the fruits of self-love. Have confidence, My child. Do not lose heart in coming for pardon, for I am always ready to forgive you. As often as you beg for it, you glorify My mercy" (*Diary*, 1488).

Think about forgiveness and the story of St. Mary Magdalene. An accomplished sinner, she initially washed, kissed, and anointed the feet of Jesus out of contrition, and after His death, out of devotion. In spite of her past sins, she loved Jesus very much and stayed with Mother Mary during the crucifixion. (See John 19:25.) It was not Peter, or His beloved disciple John, who was the first to the tomb and who announced the Resurrection. No, it was Mary Magdalene! What great hope that should give us!

TRUE FORGIVENESS

Forgiveness is an act of the will. It is not a feeling. It does not erase the memories of what happened, and does not trivialize the sin. Forgiveness is not amnesia, and is not the same as forgetting what happened. Forgiveness is not about erasing the memory, rather, about healing of the memory.

The *Catechism of the Catholic Church* says this about forgiveness:

> Thus the Lord's words on forgiveness, the love that loves to the end, become a living reality. The parable of the merciless servant, which crowns the Lord's teaching on ecclesial communion, ends with these words: "So also my heavenly Father will do to every one of you, if you do not forgive your brother from your heart." It is there, in fact, "in the depths of the heart," that everything is bound and loosed. It is not in our power not to feel or to forget an offense; but the heart that offers itself to the Holy Spirit turns injury into compassion and purifies the memory in transforming the hurt into intercession (#2843).

As you experience His mercy, realize that you are called to be a vessel of that mercy to others. For every abortion, many people are responsible. If you have asked forgiveness for your part, ask God to forgive all the others who were responsible as well. This may include some or all of the following people: the other parent of the aborted child; family members who pushed for the abortion or who simply did nothing to help; friends who gave advice of despair, saying abortion was the only option; the doctors, nurses, escorts, and counselors at the abortion clinic, who thought they were doing something helpful; the clergy who were afraid to say anything; the people who, after the abortion, made light of it and said not to feel bad, as if the child were no more than tissue.

And by making the effort to forgive, a slow healing process begins and deep internal wounds begin to heal. We start the long trek on "the long and winding road" to spiritual, psychological, and emotional good health. But we must believe that God loves and forgives the sinner.

CHAPTER 7
Healing Comes through the Church

JESUS CAME FOR SINNERS

All throughout the New Testament are passages where Jesus healed lepers (Lk 5:12-13), paralytics, (Lk 5:18-25) rebuked spirits and those spiritually ill (Lk 6:18, 9:42), and even raised the dead (Mk 5:35-42; Jn 11:1-53). When asked why He dined with tax collectors and sinners, He replied, *"Those who are well have no need of a physician, but those who are sick; I have not come to call the righteous, but sinners to repentance"* (Lk 5:30-32). Jesus did not condemn the woman caught in the act of adultery. Rather, He told her to, *"Go, and do not sin again"* (Jn 8:11).

We know that killing an unborn child is wrong, yet, for many women, the difficult decision faced and the feelings of confusion, helplessness, despair, and anxiety during the time that led to the decision is understood. In his encyclical letter *Evangelium Vitae* (The *Gospel of Life*), paragraph 99, Pope John Paul II had a special message for women who have had an abortion:

> The Church is aware of the many factors, which may have influenced your decision, and she does not doubt that in many cases it was a painful and even shattering decision. The wound in your heart may not yet have healed. Certainly what happened was and remains terribly wrong. But do not give in to discour-

agement and do not lose hope. Try rather to understand what happened and face it honestly. If you have not already done so, give yourselves over with humility and trust to repentance. The Father of mercies is ready to give you His forgiveness and His peace in the Sacrament of Reconciliation. To the same Father and to His mercy you can with sure hope entrust your child.

In the book *Crossing the Threshhold of Hope*, Pope John Paul II writes:

> … We are witnessing true human tragedies. Often the woman is the victim of male selfishness, in the sense that the man, who has contributed to the conception of new life, does not want to be burdened with it and leaves the responsibility to the woman, as if it were "her fault" alone. So, precisely, when the woman most needs the man's support, he proves to be a cynical egotist, capable of exploiting her affection or weakness, yet stubbornly resistant to any sense of responsibility for his action.

IT IS A BIG DEAL

The message of the Church in the midst of all this strikes the perfect balance both psychologically and spiritually. There are two things that the post-abortive woman does not need to hear. One is: "It's no big deal." In reality, she knows abortion is a big deal and experiences a natural grief for her child who has been killed. Yet many in society make her feel silly for feeling sad. Her grief, therefore, cannot be adequately expressed and processed. The process is short-circuited. Moreover, she may well be quite angry with those whose message about "no big deal" got her into the mess of abortion in the first place. To hear that message again, and to be given more excuses, is the last thing she needs. This is one reason why church bodies that take a "pro-choice" position become ill-equipped to deal with those who suffer from an abortion.

But Don't Condemn

The second thing the post-abortive woman does not need is someone who will condemn her and drive her deeper into the despair, which the act of abortion is all too capable of generating on its own.

The message of the Catholic Church and of the pro-life movement avoids both of these harmful ideas. Our clear identification of abortion as an evil, which is never morally licit, corresponds with the deepest truth she is hearing in her mind and heart. It cuts through the rhetoric, empty excuses, and terrible pressures others have heaped upon her. It breaks through denial and assures her she has a reason for her grief.

Then at the same time and in the same breath, we give the message of hope. The doors of the Church are open. We are not here to reject or condemn, but to welcome back to the peace and mercy of Christ whomever has been involved in abortion. One of the authors (FP) knows of someone who had 24 abortions. Yet, even she can be forgiven! We long to welcome her back, and so does the God of mercy.

CONFESSION IS KEY TO HEALING

For Catholic men and women, the Sacrament of Reconciliation must be at the heart of the healing process.

> Those who approach the Sacrament of Penance obtain pardon from God's mercy for the offenses committed against Him, and are, at the same time, reconciled with the Church which they have wounded by their sins and which by charity, by example, and by prayer labors for their conversion (*CCC*, 1422). It is called the *sacrament of forgiveness*, since by the priest's sacramental absolution God grants the penitent "pardon and peace" (*CCC*, 1449).

We must come to know and understand the forgiveness of God and others. However, we must also learn to forgive ourselves. Through the Sacrament of Reconciliation, your sin has been forgiven and you have been made new in Christ. We must trust in God and turn the children over to the care of the Great Physician. Below the Image of The Divine Mercy are the words "Jesus, I trust in You!" Let us strive harder each day to turn our guilt and shame, our worries and anxieties over to Him, for He can turn our sadness into joy!

So today, we implore all of you, but especially

those who have been caught up in the evil of abortion, to come back to Him, the Merciful Savior. And also know that God loves you just as you are, and that He came to heal the sinner, not the upright. Let us take to heart and find comfort in the words of Our Lord to St. Faustina: "**The greater the sinner, the greater the right to My mercy**" (*Diary*, 723). Those who have committed the greatest sins have the greatest right to His mercy!

CHURCH: VEHICLE FOR HEALING

Because the Church is the vehicle for healing, the priest has a key role to play. He is an ambassador of God's mercy. One of the common concerns clergy have in regard to speaking about abortion is that they "don't want to hurt the women in the congregation who have had abortions." They feel that the presence of such women is a reason to be silent about it. But just the opposite is true. Experts in post-abortion syndrome tell us that the first step toward healing is to break out of denial, and silence does not help to do that. The woman suffering from abortion may think we are silent because we do not know her pain, do not care, or have no hope to offer. In truth, however, we speak because we do know, do care, and do offer hope.

The process of healing is delicate and long. Sometimes it begins with pain. The availability of compassionate post-abortion counselors in the parish goes a long way. Clergy, moreover, should see that truth and compassion are not at odds with one another. To withhold the truth is to lack compassion because compassion seeks to meet the needs of the other, and we have a need for truth. At the same time, to lack compassion is to withhold an aspect of the truth of the Gospel and the Church. In God, truth and love are ultimately one, for He Himself is both.

When the priest proclaims the gift of life and the mercy of God, and then is available to reconcile sinners in the Sacrament of Penance, people will be uplifted and healed.

CHAPTER 8
Turning the Lies into Truth
Great Signs of Hope

The triumph of mercy over abortion is seen also in the lives of those who used to actually perform and advocate abortion, and have repented. They bring to life the words of Our Lord to St. Faustina, **"The greater the sinner, the greater the right he has to My mercy"** (*Diary*, 723).

'ROE NO MORE'

We mentioned earlier the devastating effects of *Roe vs. Wade*. Yet the plaintiff of that case, the "Jane Roe" herself, is now pro-life! Norma McCorvey has repented of her sins, been baptized, and joined the Catholic Church. She now works full-time for an end to abortion and the healing of those who have been wounded by it.

Norma became the "Jane Roe" of *Roe vs. Wade* because she thought that the attorneys in her hometown of Dallas could help her. Pregnant for the third time, she did not feel she could continue the pregnancy. Yet, when her doctor mentioned the word "abortion" to her, she had to look it up in the dictionary. Finding out that it was not legal, and wondering what she could do, she was referred to attorneys Sarah Weddington and Linda Coffee, who were looking for ways to overturn the abortion restrictions in Texas law.

Norma was used. She put her name to the necessary papers because she thought she would be helped. She was not helped, nor was she kept informed of the progress of her "case" in any substantive way. She never had an abortion, because it was not possible to overturn the law so quickly. Three years later, she found out about the decision in the *Roe vs. Wade* case just like everyone else did. She technically had won, but there was no joy for her.

IN THE INDUSTRY BUT NOT OF IT

She stayed anonymous. Eventually, however, she revealed her identity and began speaking publicly for the pro-abortion movement. She also began working in an abortion facility in Dallas. Yet, being so close to the industry that she helped legalize began to disillusion her. One afternoon, for example, a patient said she was too nervous to fill out the intake form. When another patient chimed in and said abortion was "just like getting a tooth pulled," Norma objected. She began to explain to the nervous patient the step-by-step facts of the procedure. Norma then urged her to be sure of what she was doing, telling her she did not want her to get hurt. The girl decided not to go through with the abortion.

Unmerited grace was already at work in Norma's heart and mind. She had more loyalty to the moms than to the abortionist. At the same time, Operation Rescue moved its national headquarters next door to the abortion mill. Day by day, Norma's stereotypes of the pro-life activists were dismantled. Far from being self-righteous, dangerous fanatics, they showed themselves kind, loving, and ready to embrace her. In fact, a key moment in Norma's discovery of mercy was the moment she was asked to give it. Rev. Flip Benham, director of Operation Rescue, approached Norma one day and asked forgiveness for some unkind words he had spoken to her in public at a recent event. "I'm sorry," he said, "Will you forgive me?" Norma was astonished. Why was this happening? This is the man who is opposed to everything I do, she thought. Doesn't he regard me as evil? How can he be asking me for forgiveness? She excused herself, went back into the abortion mill, and wept. Divine Mercy was at work.

Norma learned that Christians can separate the sin from the sinner, and she began to learn to do that too. She saw that the Christians wanted to get to know her, and to take her to Church. The little daughter of one of the Rescue members invited Norma over and over, and she eventually had to say yes to this child's unconditional love. She began to see that the fact that pro-life people *condemned what she did* was not the same as condemning *her*. This distinction between the *problem* and the *person* helped her to eventually see that a crisis pregnancy did not mean that the *baby* was the problem. Indeed, the *baby* was a person, deserving respect despite any unfavorable circumstances.

The love of Christians led Norma to the waters

of Baptism in 1995. The reality of "new life in Christ" became the centerpiece of her existence, and she strove to live accordingly. She started a ministry called *Roe No More*, through which she is able to write, speak, and counsel many women to choose life.

LED TO THE CHURCH

Having had exposure to Catholicism in her early life, Norma began asking Fr. Frank Pavone questions about the Catholic faith, and felt herself drawn by the beauty of the Church's liturgy and teachings. In 1998, she made her profession of faith and became a Catholic. She writes the following about that day:

I started getting cold chills right before I went up for my First Holy Communion. I knew somehow that it was the Holy Spirit. Then when I received the flesh of Christ's Body and His Blood, I felt a real sense of inner peace. After Communion, Fr. Frank shared the following words that spoke directly to my heart:

Norma, reflect carefully on what has happened now that you have received Jesus for the first time in Holy Communion.

Our faith teaches that by His Incarnation, the Son of God joined all humanity to Himself. In some fashion, every human being of all time is united to Him. This, of course, includes every human being in the womb, and includes those who were aborted.

Today, you have received the very same flesh of the Son of God, to which all humanity has been joined. That means, Norma, that today, in giving you His Body, Jesus has also given you back all the babies that were aborted because of what you did. He has reunited to you all the children who never got to play in the playgrounds. He has restored them to you, closing the distance between you and them. He has reconciled them to you and given you peace.

The first time I ever interviewed you, I started by saying, "So, you are the Jane Roe of Roe vs. Wade.*" You responded, "No, Father, I was the Jane Roe of* Roe vs. Wade.*" Norma, those words were never truer than they are today. Amen.*

During these remarks, I was sitting there crying. I knew I had been forgiven — and to think I was reunited with those children … it was sorrow and joy at the same time. It was like having my own children come back to me all at one time. It was like seeing all their faces, even though I've never known them. (From *My Journey into the Catholic Church*, by Norma McCorvey and Fr. Frank Pavone)

A PRO-ABORTION LEADER CONVERTS

Divine Mercy is also triumphant in the life of Dr. Bernard Nathanson, who was a key architect of the abortion-rights movement, a co-founder of the National Abortion Rights Action League (NARAL), ran the largest abortion facility in the Western world, and even aborted his own child. He too now drinks from the fountain of God's mercy in the Sacraments of the Church.

Ironically, it was precisely the Church and its hierarchy that Nathanson and his colleagues targeted in their strategy to uncage the abortion monster. They knew that the Church was the only significant obstacle in their way, and in their press releases they attempted to divide the shepherds from their flock, claiming that most Catholics approved of abortion. Moreover, Nathanson says that they took a calculated risk that the clergy would remain relatively silent. "We would never have gotten away with what we did," he has said to priests, "if you had been united, purposeful, and strong." He claims that he and his colleagues "stole the abortion issue from the Church" while the Church was sleeping.

Dr. Nathanson was the director of the Center for Reproductive and Sexual Health in New York City. In his two years in that position, he oversaw some 60,000 abortions. He also supervised residents in training who performed another 10,000 abortions. In addition, he performed some 5,000 abortions with his own hands in private practice.

Dr. Nathanson even aborted *his own child*. He writes in *The Hand of God*:

I believe it was Father Zossima in *The Brothers Karamazov*, who defined hell as the suffering of one unable to love, and if this is true, I have served my sentence and then some. What is it like to terminate the life of your own child? It was aseptic and clinical. Yes, you may ask me but how did you feel? Did you not feel sad — not only because you had extinguished the life of an unborn child, but more, because you had destroyed your own child? I swear to you that I had no feelings aside from the sense of accomplishment, the pride of expertise. On inspecting the contents of the bag I felt only the satisfaction of knowing that I had done a thorough job. You pursue me: You ask if perhaps for a fleeting moment or so I experienced a flicker of regret, a microgram of remorse? No and no. And that, dear reader, is the mentality of the abortionist: another job well done, another demonstration of the moral neutrality of advanced technology in the hands of the amoral (pp. 58-61).

SCIENTIFIC DOUBT

Yet, during his practice of abortion, Dr. Nathanson became increasingly unable to reconcile the contradiction between the sometimes-heroic medical efforts to save prematurely delivered babies and the legal slaughter of babies at the very same stage of development in the very same building. This, coupled with the increasing knowledge science was gaining about the human embryo and fetus, caused him to doubt, *from a purely scientific stance*, whether abortion was advisable. In fact, he began wondering whether he had, in fact, presided over the deaths of 75,000 human beings.

God is the God of *all* truth, not simply religious truth. Divine Mercy was reaching out to Bernard Nathanson through his perception of the natural truths of science and logic. It also reached him through the witness of pro-life activism. At a Planned Parenthood clinic on Manhattan's Lower East Side, he witnessed 1,200 Operation Rescue demonstrators wrapping their arms around each other, singing hymns, smiling at the police and the media. He was writing a magazine article on the morality of clinic blockades. He circled about the demonstrators, doing interviews, taking notes, and observing the faces. "It was only then," he writes in his book *The Hand of God*, "that I apprehended the exaltation, the pure love on the faces of that shivering mass of people, surrounded as they were by hundreds of New York City policemen." He listened as they prayed for the unborn, the women seeking abortions, the doctors and nurses in the clinic, the police, and reporters covering the event. "They prayed for each other but never for themselves," he writes. "And I wondered: How can these people give of themselves for a constituency that is (and always will be) mute, invisible, and unable to thank them? It was only then," he adds, "that I began seriously to question what indescribable Force generated them to this activity."

That "Force" became more and more palpable and personal as Dr. Nathanson, now as a pro-life agnostic, began speaking to more and more pro-life groups. He states that the warmth and love of the pro-life people is what began to break through the shell of his agnosticism. Coming to know the love and mercy of Christians, he came to know the God they worship.

FREED FROM SIN

Eventually, with the kind help and guidance of Fr. John McCloskey, an Opus Dei priest based in Princeton, New Jersey, Dr. Nathanson felt drawn to the waters of Baptism in the Catholic Church. Cardinal John O'Connor, Archbishop of New York, and a leading voice in the pro-life movement baptized him into the Church. "I am free from my sin," Dr. Nathanson says. "For the first time in my life, I will feel the shelter and warmth of faith" (Julia Duin, *Crisis Magazine*, June 1996).

Today, Dr. Nathanson lives his life as a faithful Catholic who knows, as well as anyone else, what the mercy of God means to a sinner. He has also become a bioethicist, and a key focus of his studies has been the meaning of "dignity" as the "Imago Dei," the *image of God*, in which every human life is created. Through his speaking, he tries to awaken the Church to another threat: *the genetic tampering with the human species*. What is at stake, he points out, is the very meaning of being human, and the survival and destiny of humanity.

Dr. Nathanson is not the only one to come out of the abortion industry. Thousands of others have done so and continue to do so each day. Many of them have formed an international association through which they seek their spiritual and psychological healing. The name of this organization is the "Society of Centurions." Just as the Centurion at the Cross repented of his participation in the death of Jesus, who was innocent, so these men and women now repent of having killed innocent babies. Many of them even pledge to contact the women on whom they have performed abortions and apologize to them, and help them find healing. These former abortionists have experienced God's mercy, and they want to help the women whom they harmed to experience it as well. They also want other abortionists to experience it, and have established an outreach called the "Prodigal Project." In this effort, pro-life people present to abortion facility workers a brochure, written by former abortionists, that invites the workers to leave the industry of death behind, and to find forgiveness and a normal life.

How great is God's mercy, which can transform and heal the abortionists themselves and can transform our entire society into a Society of Centurions!

CHAPTER 9
Leading the Way in Repentance

'PRAY FOR US SINNERS'

Those who are active in the pro-life movement are called to be prophets of justice for the unborn, and also prophets of mercy for those guilty of abortion. None of us is a stranger to temptation and sin; we have all aborted God's will in our lives. To stand up for the unborn, then, is not an act of self-righteousness.

In fact, it is an act of repentance. Think, for example, of what pro-life people say when they pray in front of an abortion facility. In the *Our Father* we say, "Forgive us *our* trespasses." In the *Hail Mary* we say, "Pray for *us sinners*." And in the Chaplet of Divine Mercy, before we invoke that mercy "on the whole world," we say, "Have mercy *on us*."

We, who stand up for life, first of all ask forgiveness for our own inaction, our own silence, and our own unwillingness to help others. Then, from this posture of repentance, we can implore the Lord to end abortion, and can implore our neighbor to respect the lives of our tiniest neighbors. We who oppose abortion do not oppose those who have abortions; rather, we embrace them with love. We do not simply say, "Abortion is wrong — don't do it." We say what Christ says to us: "I am with you. I will reach out my hand to give you the strength to rise from sin and do what is right."

Being Proactive with Truth

A prophet is one who speaks the Truth. We must be proactive in educating an uneducated society on the horrors of abortion. So many know so little on the effects of a promiscuous lifestyle, and many even less on the *in utero* development of the growing child in the mother's womb.

There are other small things that we can do to promote a culture of life and one of respect for woman and motherhood. We should encourage and promote chastity to our youth, and help them understand the sanctity of marriage and the concept of what the word *commitment* really means. We should decry the proliferation of pornography – something that promotes the notion that women are little more than sexual objects to be used for male pleasure, and "if it feels good, then do it." And we should be proactive in eliminating violence in the media. Our children are being numbed by the constant barrage of violence on television, in the movies, and in the music they enjoy. The saying, "what you eat, you become," also holds true for the foods of sex and violence that we use to feed our brains and numb our spirits.

We must be voices crying out in the desert, and not be afraid to give words of encouragement to parents who have large families. We can give support to those struggling in their marriage to obtain the needed help and save the relationship. Marriage today is not looked on as a lifelong commitment, and spouses typically do not take each other "for better or worse." When troubles arise, divorce is often the outcome, and this only propagates the dysfunction so common in families today.

All of these factors and many more interplay together to create an environment of promiscuity, violence, and a lack of commitment. Yet, we should be icons of mercy to a hurting world, especially to those grieving over the loss of their aborted child. Since we know that God is love, all things done should be done out of love and not anger.

CHAPTER 10
Trust and the Divine Mercy Message

TURNING OVER CONTROL

Jesus asked that the words "Jesus, I trust in You!" be inscribed below the image of The Divine Mercy. Trust is the virtue that is the foundation and essence of those desiring to live the message of Divine Mercy. We are to be vessels of mercy, and how much this vessel can hold and radiate out to others depends on trust. There is much more to trust than believing God is trustworthy: We must act on that belief and turn control of our lives over to Him. Trust requires a conversion of the heart and soul and gives us the wisdom to understand the need to ask for His mercy, be merciful to others, and let Him be in charge. True peace will then reign in our hearts.

The Lord made it clear to Saint Faustina that the more we trust in Him and strive to live His will and not ours, the more graces we will receive. He told her, **"Tell [all people], My daughter, that I am Love and Mercy itself. When a soul approaches Me with trust, I fill it with such an abundance of graces that it cannot contain them within itself, but radiates them to other souls"** (*Diary*, 1074).

On another occasion He told her,

> Let souls who are striving for perfection particularly adore My mercy, because the

abundance of graces which I grant them flows from My mercy. I desire that these souls distinguish themselves by boundless trust in My mercy. I Myself will attend to the sanctification of such souls. I will provide them with everything they will need to attain sanctity. The graces of My mercy are drawn by means of one vessel only, and that is trust. The more a soul trusts, the more it will receive. Souls that trust boundlessly are a great comfort to Me, because I pour all the treasures of My graces into them. I rejoice that they ask for much, because it is My desire to give much, very much. On the other hand, I am sad when souls ask for little, when they narrow their hearts (*Diary*, 1578).

LACK OF TRUST DENIES US MERCY

The Lord wants us to trust in His mercy. So, when we sin and falter, we must humble ourselves and ask for His mercy. Intertwined with a lack of trust in God, who is Love and Mercy itself, many of us carry guilt, anger, shame, and lack of forgiveness in our souls. We ponder, "How could God ever forgive me?" But we are not unique in our disbelief. In a powerful testimony of His mercy, St. Faustina wrote,

> On the evening of the last day before my departure for Vilnius, an elderly sister revealed the condition of her soul to me. She said that she had already been suffering interiorly for several years, that it seemed to her that all her

confessions had been bad, and that she had doubts as to whether the Lord Jesus had forgiven her. I asked her if she had ever told her confessor about this. She answered that she had spoken many times about this to her confessors and ... "The confessors are always telling me to be at peace, but I still suffer very much, and nothing brings me relief, and it constantly seems to me that God has not forgiven me." I answered, "You should obey your confessor, Sister, and be fully at peace, because this is certainly a temptation."

But she entreated me with tears in her eyes to ask Jesus if He had forgiven her and whether her confessions had been good or not. I answered forcefully, "Ask Him yourself, Sister, if you don't believe your confessors!" But she clutched my hand and did not want to let go until I gave her an answer, and she kept asking me to pray for her and let her know what Jesus would tell me about her. Crying bitterly, she would not let me go and said to me, "I know that the Lord Jesus speaks to you, Sister." Since she was clutching my hand and I could not wrench myself away, I promised her I would pray for her. In the evening, during Benediction, I heard these words in my soul: **"Tell her that her disbelief wounds My heart more than the sins she committed."** When I told her this, she began to cry like a child, and great joy entered her soul. I understood that God wanted to console this soul through me.

Even though it cost me a great deal, I fulfilled God's wish (*Diary*, 628).

Reflect on His words; "Tell her that her disbelief wounds My heart more than the sins she committed." When we confess our sins and show remorse, there is no reason to carry guilt and shame, because He is the Great Physician. He can heal our wounds and scarred hearts. St. Faustina wrote, "Today, the Lord said to me, '**I have opened My Heart as a living fountain of mercy. Let all souls draw life from it. Let them approach this sea of mercy with great trust. Sinners will attain justification, and the just will be confirmed in good. Whoever places his trust in My mercy will be filled with My divine peace at the hour of death**" (*Diary*, 1520). The writer of Hebrews tells us, *"Let us therefore approach the throne of grace with boldness, so that we may receive mercy and find grace to help in time of need"* (4:16).

MARY, OUR MODEL

When the angel Gabriel visited Our Blessed Mother, Mary's reply was *"Behold, I am the handmaid of the Lord; let it be to me according to Your word"* (Lk 1:36). And at a young age, she found herself pregnant and unmarried. Imagine her faith when the Holy Family had to flee to Egypt or her faith that was tested as she watched Jesus be scourged and crucified.

In our own lives, trust in God is easy wh things are going well. However, in times of tr doubt appears and we wonder "Where is God?" or "Does He really exist?" We look at apparent obstacles with our human eyes, and wonder if we will ever get through all the struggles of life, let alone cope with all our past mistakes. If we pray, discern, and believe we are doing His will, then we must ask for fortitude and strength and a deeper faith. In times of struggle and frustration, we should have the attitude of Peter, who said, *"'Master, we have worked all night long but have caught nothing. Yet if You say so, I will let down the nets.' When they had done this, they caught so many fish that their nets were beginning to break. So they signaled their partners in the other boat to come and help them"* (Lk 5:5-7). This attitude obviously requires great faith. However, in times of trial our faith is tested and that is when we must trust in Him. As spiritual warriors, we must *"walk by faith, not by sight"* (2 Cor 5:7).

So today, let us thank God for His unfathomable mercy. Know that broken as we all are, God loves us unconditionally and just the way we are. All of us are called to be the light of the world, bringing the message of mercy to a hurting and broken humanity. Let us use our mistakes as a vehicle for conversion and evangelization, letting he Rays of Mercy from The Divine Mercy radiate us, through us, and out to the rest of the world.